ROBERT L. SMITH

# REFRACTIONS

DRAGON'S TEETH PRESS

REFRACTIONS
First Edition


Published by Dragon's Teeth Press
El Dorado National Forest
Georgetown, California 95634
Manufactured in the United States of America

LIBRARY OF CONGRESS CATALOG CARD NUMBER: 79-53012

COVER DESIGN BY NANCY SMITH

ACKNOWLEDGEMENTS

"Ten Eye-Blinks on the Beach" appeared in the *Martha's Vineyard Gazette*. "The Toy Monkey" will appear in a future issue of *The Laurel Review*. "Autumn" appeared in *Scimitar and Song*. "Stations of the Zoo" appeared in *Descant*. "Seven Couplets With Crotchets" appeared in the *Wormwood Review*. "Don Juan Says Farewell" appeared in *The Beloit Poetry Journal*. "Among the Clocks" appeared in *Gone Soft*. "Shaft and Target" appeared in *Stone Country*. "Cautionary Tale" appeared in the *Mississippi Review*. "Three Stages" appeared in *Green River Review*, Spring-Summer, 1978. Thanks are due the editors for permission to reprint.

LIVING POETS SERIES
Number 21
Available at $3.50
from

DRAGON'S TEETH PRESS
El Dorado National Forest
Georgetown, California 95634

ISBN 0-934218-11-0

NTENTS

## FOREWORD

Robert L. Smith's first collection of poems presents its readers an already developed talent. Here is a matured sensibility and a speaking voice that is unaffected and graceful with a wide range of subjects and meters. We will sometimes be almost overwhelmed by the poetry's technical control, high-powered wit, and avoidance of obvious or heavy ironies. But mainly what is felt throughout is the great fun Smith has in the charging of language. This individual language both carries the subject and supports complex emotions:

*The point where I would puncture you is always*
*Somewhere else. I'd liefer fire a maser*
*At the moon to hit a moving microbe*
*Than try to put an arrow through your apple.*

*Wind and weather, whim and circumstance*
*Keep my bolts enquivered and intact.*
    *But oh those days how sweet! When the bullseye ring*
    *Falls to perfect circle with the other thing.*

*(Shaft and Target)*

Even when the subject is affection and true sentiment, the voice retains its witty, often oblique quality. In the last part of "Three Stages," before the final crescendo, the voice cries:

*You: were You, dark, against the cloud*
        *in a V of buoyant wingbeats*
    *were You tiny chirp-and-shadow*
        *in the trees*

and the viewing continues–almost objective–until the unabashed clincher, "I would hold you."

Despite the intermittent sense of play, serious things are being spoken of, and many times the observations are grim. In one poem, "He knows that breath/Itself's an illness, which the dark will mend." And, in another:

*That we, poor quivering mites, are clustered on*
*A ball of warmth caught up in a galactic*
*Royal Progress; scrabbling on a gobbet*

*Of dung as we squeak and eat each other.*

*(Don Juan Says Farewell)*

But this knowledge elicits from Smith muted irony and humor, not tones of despair.

Much of the rich humor will be found in poems which have animals at the metaphoric center, such "Cautionary Tale," "25 Blackouts 25," "What the Gull Said," and "Stations of the Zoo." In these poems especially we are always on the verge of a joke, albeit one with a moral center. From "Ten Things I Will Not Do," one is "Collect!/Sand-grains in a snuffbox/Beans in a jar/Money." Another is, "Count the stars in an interstice of leaves," and yet another is, "Decide which is 'Will not'/And what is 'Must not.'" These three, as do all of the ten, provide differing tones, finely balanced.

Any taint of loaded didacticism is obliterated by Robert Smith's often distanced, humorous voice, and his concentration on the image, on what is specific and real. He imagines a toy monkey running down "lifeless":

*I could have changed his batteries, I suppose,*
*But what he was was what I loved, waning*
*Though it was.*

*(The Toy Monkey)*

Note the shift in pronoun, note the thoroughgoing empathy with the image conjured by a toy. The poem, through its warmth and emotion, earns its extravagant last words: "Does he dream? Do I?" The very sure focus on the visual causes the language to sing here, as it does elsewhere, for instance at the close of "Autumn," a lyric of classical precision.

Whatever his subject, the messages are all absorbed in the physical, in what the poet sees and, graciously, allows us to see.

—Dr. Barry Wallenstein
Assistant Professor of English
The City College of New York

# I

## TO E.

I took Resentment by the hand
        And cared for it
As though it were a child.

I fed it peanut-crunch and cyclamates
        And dressed it in the neatest clothes
        And let it keep a horsefly-larva in a jar
        And watched with calm indulgence as
        It ripped out pages
                                        from the Book of Reason.

And when my mutterings
        Had turned it into porcelain
I put it on the shelf
        Among the others.

## THE JOGGER UNLACES HIS SHOES

My toe
Could touch the same crevice
On the same street
On the same block
Just so
After only a month's practice

Two rocking ships
ships awash
Two puffing ships
ships saluting
Two passing ships
ships off-course

I was upset to learn
That the doorman
Twelve-point-twenty minutes away
Had died.

But his awning was still there
And the building
And I was free
To try another street.

I will not ford the asphalt river
    At a driveway or a fireplug
Three decisions are too many
    For such a minor daring

It would be better
To be a watermelon

A watermelon
Will not burst
    With its own bloodstream

I attempt to make
    There Here
To make
    Here There
    Is to stop
    Altogether

## THE JUMPER

He could see
Through the haze
Ceiling's outline

Weedy water
Weighed his socks
He crouched and leapt

Kneejoints snapped
Tendons cracked
But the fire-lit

Rosy cherub
In the mantel
Grinned at him

So up again
Hand held high
Fingers spear-point

Down and up
Floor more distant
Ceiling higher

Not ceiling
But a floor
Footfalls through it

Footfalls on it
Endless footfalls
Above, below

Up and arching
Slowly settling:
Slower, slower

Equiposed
Between a leap
And a descent

Frigate-bird
'Twixt sky and sea
Desiring neither

## THE THREE SAGES

"I met Joy," the first one said,
"in a desert place. Angel with
Thin-feathered wings, he shook my hand,
Apologized, and said his circuit
Was so large that men may know
His touch but once a human lifetime."

"He is a bureaucrat," the second
Said, "with dirty glasses and
A full 'In'-box. His desk supports
Six phones, all off the hook, and I
Suspect his secretary's on
Eternal coffee-break. He said
He'd start my application soon.
I almost asked him for a driver's
License, or a blood test, or
A passport, or a Sign of Life,
Until I saw his 'Out'-box, with
The forms stamped 'Joy is Terminated',
And I turned and hurried out."

"Anthropomorphics," said the third.
"Joy's a neat conjunction of
Two lines, and the destruction of
The one straight endless; the conviction
That the stars are eyes, and leaves
A green and soft applause; the holding
Of a corselet-link whose tint
Is blood shed more than twice one hundred
Thousand days ago; fingers
Burnishing themselves like bell-notes

Shaken in a crystal vial;
The micro-second of contentment
During drunkenness; the twinge
Of apprehension dropped upon
Our lids at Sleep's slow advent, and
The reassuring tug of Waking."

# AMONG THE CLOCKS

## I

### *Ticks*

Butterfly's wingbeat
        Tick
Of its one month of life
Locust's chirr
        Tick
Of seventeen years released at once
Man's lifetime
        Tick
Of a bubble bursting in Communion wine
Wavebreak
        Tick
In the shifting truce of land and sea

## II

### *Chimes*

Earth
        rings
            at every temblor

Harmonic of
        the sun's
            deep note

Mid-tone of
the infinite
Westminster sequence

Lappet-ball
of a Reindeer
grazing on an endless tundra

Pendant on a glockenspiel
played
by a demented Bear

III

*The Sundial*

does not keep time

Rather
a combination-lock
upon the vault of hours

Rather
a switch
that shuts off dawn and dusk

Rather
a magma-dike
uncovered in the tides of light

Rather
        the fin of a basking dolphin
              in the slow whirlpool of days and nights

Rather
        a lily-iron
              too small to hold the diving Earth

## IV

The hammer falls the
Chimes resound their last the
Hands that lit the
Phosphor numerals for men long vanished
        Slow and stop
        Beneath the dust
Drawn to the last warmth's
              Final shudder

## TEN EYE-BLINKS ON THE BEACH

I

Skate-egg cases: small black sleds left by sea-brine children.

II

Is it a house there, where the eave projects grey-silver shingles
from the sand?

III

A bottle, frosted soft, the mold from which all bottles came.

IV

A tree-branch: tentacles from some lost monster's frozen corpse.

V

White sand-fleas with black eye-dots: darting microbes on a
windy agar-plate.

VI

Something in the bleached crab-shell peers out through
intact eye-stalks.

VII

Dry globules clumped in an amber cauliflower, or an emptied
brain.

VIII

A small ambassador, badly briefed on his new post, lies askew
and milky-eyed at surf's edge.

IX

Starfish, curly-flanged and tan, strewn like brittle breakfast
food.

X

The gull, self-appointed Custodian, picks his way through
his littoral Museum.

## WHAT THE GULL SAID

I won't tell you what he said.
He was flying overhead
        With another
        Nestling brother
Talking confidentially.

And what I chanced to overhear
Made it miserably clear
        That Life is brief
        And filled with grief
And that's no news to you and me.

## CAUTIONARY TALE

Once there was a large-type primate (let's say
Gorilla) who got sick and bloody
Tired of bananas and runny fruit
And a chilly concrete floor for his
Behind, and screaming kids with their damn balloons
And nobody to talk to but sparrows
Who never listened anyway. So one day
He snitched a keeper's toilet-kit and in
The night shaved with the electric razor
(Don't ask how come electricity
In his cage – just read on) all over,
And loped out through the Park and scared some poor
Wight clean out of his clothes with his bow legs
And blue-white skin and loose little paunch and
Nose you could see clear into. Now it's Clothes
That Make the Man, and sure enough, by
The time he got to Fifth Avenue and
The place where policemen dwell he looked just like
Any other everyday round-shouldered
Man with a touch of acromegaly.
He got a job with the U.S. Post Office
Where his simian arms came in handy,
And found a room private enough to hang
A tire from the ceiling, and spent his
Money on razor blades and succulents.

He began to get about some, and
Joined a "Y" where he slung the barbells
Around and did beautifully on the high
Bar; but he couldn't be lured into
The swimming-pool. At parties he had his
Prehensile big toes woefully stepped on
While he devastated the snack-trays
(Especially those with celery), and was thought
An attentive if taciturn guest,
Illustrating the enormous truth
That a good listener ne'er goes hors d'oeuvre-less.
Still and all, he felt left out somehow, for
The people he met here and there were so
Full of voting rights for Negroes and
Mars shots and electronic tonal-
ities and Paint-Splattered versus Paint-trickled
That sometimes he thought wistfully of a
Particularly drowsy patch of summer
Sunlight in the corner of his old cage.
He got out some books from the library.
He read Aristotle's "Politics" and
Machiavelli and Thucydides;
And Proust and Shakespeare and "Saki" and Adam
Smith; and listened to Beethoven and
John Cage recordings and went to galleries

And remembered the chimpanzee down
The aisle who'd done finger-paintings and gotten
On TV. And went to a party
All primed and ready to talk. And after
He had discoursed for awhile and several
People had come, several people had
Walked away, and several people had
Left the party altogether, he
Happened to catch sight of himself in
The mirror over the punchbowl, and thought
That his forehead was much higher and
His arms looked quite short and his baggy clothes
Seemed to fit, and that he hadn't a
Notion of what he'd been saying, but
That was all right because no one seemed
To notice. So he went home and slept a
Quiet night with a smile on his muzzle.

## CELESTIAL PRESS CONFERENCE
(*In Which He Answers Questions of Importance*)

Q: Who was the First Man?
A: The first to ask that question.
Q: Who was the First Woman?
A: The second to ask that question.
Q: Is there Original Sin?
A: Rarely.
Q: When did the Universe begin?
A: When the one before ended.
Q: When will the Universe end?
A: When the next one begins.
Q: When will the next one begin?
A: When you, and I, are dead.
Q: Is there a Heaven?
A: If you want one.
Q: Is there a Hell?
A: If you want one.
Q: *I* don't believe in either.
A: You made each for yourself: as a reward for effort;
as a punishment for discourtesy and sloth. But you'll
never decide which is which.

# II

## SHAFT AND TARGET

The point where I would puncture you is always
Somewhere else. I'd liefer fire a maser
At the moon to hit a moving microbe
Than try to put an arrow through *your* apple.

Wind and weather, whim and circumstance
Keep my bolts enquivered and intact.
        But oh those days how sweet! When the bullseye ring
        Falls to perfect circle with the other thing.

## THREE STAGES

### I

### *In the Valley*

When the sun was high, the birds were still,
And we dozed beneath the sussurant leaves.
We swam away our drowsing in the pool,
And counted water spiders as they bobbed
And skittered on our waves. You wrung your hair dry
On the bank, and combed it to your knees,
And when you tossed your head to send it rippling
Down your back, the sun glanced auburn highlights
From your hair and brows.
          One day of many such.

From the rock that split the waves, I threw
The net and pulled it up onto the beach.
We chased the silver fish, laughing as
They slipped between our fingers. We ate them
Fresh and raw, the tiny silver fish,
Before they died upon the sand. You climbed
A palm (although we knew it was taboo)
And threw down coconuts, and when we'd
Drunk the milk, we made love in the monkeys'
Way, and slept beneath the palm.
          One day of many such.

One day we walked among the idols, green
With moss and lizards, and we asked them who
Had worshipped them before we came, and if
Their fealty (and ours) brought greater joy.
There was no answer, neither lightning nor
A heightening of blood, and I picked out
The most ferocious visage, jaguar-head
Upon a human frame, and prayed with mocking
Genuflection. You picked up a tiny
One, and spanked and hugged him, calling him
Your baby.

And then
We came to Him who leaned upon the pommel
Of his sword. Silent as the others.
Silent. Silent. Saying in our own
And separate voices, "Innocence is not
A pantomime, and no one can be born
Again." We turned and fled the yellowing
Jungle and the jeering birds.

## II

### *On Your Street*

When I came onto your street
From mine, where shutters stay closed and black-intense
against the snowy clapboards
And the air smells of sea-salt and roses and honeysuckle

And the old men nod on the bench before the bus-station
And the clouds are frosted trailing breaths from out
the sea

I leaned upon the red-and-blue mailbox
And watched the daffodil cabs straddle yellow street-lines
to play King of the Road

Deep gloom outside the streetlights, along the slatless
benches and the litter-baskets smelling of fermented
soda and ablaze with yellow bees
Deep gloom canyon between the pastry-layer windows
and the yellowing gingkos.

When You appeared
Jingling Harlequin sold franks beneath a yellow-blue
umbrella!
A Panda-doll, won with well-lobbed rings, rattled black-
dot pupils when we hugged it 'twixt us
And red-green game-lights beckoned, and fruit-clusters
of balloons,
And statues of the Virgin, blue and gold and white,
And sausage-stalls, fragrant as incense
And a carousel, with horses in slow boundings 'round
Niagara Falls, the Taj Mahal, the Trylon and
Perisphere, a paddle-wheeler on the Hudson, a boy in
a blue-velvet suit with a white lace collar, his arm

around a black and square-jawed dog, a soldier in a
soup-plate helmet advancing with rifle at high port
beneath a bursting star-shell, a merman playing a lyre.

Our walk became a Progress, 'til we, unselfish,
Joined hands with all to promenade, draped in flowers,
Around the fireplugs,
Past the doorways
Past the people thronging curbs and doorways
Past applauding people
Thronging curbs and doorways.

And at the street's end, beneath a stoplight,
I turned with You to bow
But you
Had gone through and closed a door
And I was left
Among the ice-cream wrappers and half-eaten sausages
and crumpled Tarot cards, the smells of heated tar and
rotting gingko leaves, and ribbons curling 'round my
ankles like heat-starved snakes.

Garbage-trucks like white dung-beetles
moved among concessionaires pulling down their booths,
And what was left rotted on the rain-soaked sewer-grilles
And what was left was ground away
beneath the rushing daffodil cabs and green and silver buses
and the blast and swirl of Time.

III

*The Loss*

You: were You taken through the little temples
windowless among the cypresses

New-set beneath the bright fresh sod
and wilting wreaths

In a row
of stones round-topped and so alike
that I must count right count left
to place the flower

I would hold you.

You: were You, dark, against the cloud
in a V of buoyant wingbeats

were You tiny chirp-and-shadow
in the trees

One wing-flick in the covey
picking high-stepped through the cornfield
brown and yellow in the autumn

I would hold you.

You: always in your Autumn-Spring and
Winter-Summer places
were You three stars from which
I might draw lines converging here beside me

Or, better, a whole high constellation
Stars with royal names marking off
Your knees and eyes
and hips and breasts

I would hold You.

You: were You but close behind me
as we walked irate
among the cadenced wishbones

You: but You have turned away
and put yourself by choice behind
six billion other purposes
and left me in a howling endless forest
of tossing arms and legs.

## A REFLECTION

Puffing from the stairs (their pitch and not
Their number, as he told himself), he rummaged
Slowly through the turtle-shaped spitoons
And dusty leather rocking-chairs too spring-bare
To be sat in; bass-heads, fishing-reels
And jars of salted crawfish tails; hump-backed
Trunks with bands like armadilloes; leaves
Of old tobacco nearing dust in cans.

And found a mirror, set against the wall,
And looking, in its yellowed drapery, like
A cowled monk. His height, all sconce-and-scrollwork,
Freckled at the edges, glowing as from
Candles. Window on past Christmases
And school-desks with his name scrawled on them.
He saw, like headlights past a window, days
He'd spent with friends he'd made on airplanes, on
The Grand Bahama, Sinnot's pub in Dublin,
At dinners notable for wines.
He saw
The wedding when her eyes were stony as
In Best Man Vest and jollying the Groom,
He let him know that he wore horns already.
The mirror darkened as he said, "Come *on*!
Let me talk. I herewith offer here

And herewith: Soul! All unencumbered, free
From liens and barnacles and other growths.
I have always, at my door, wiped it
Clean before I entered; hung it neatly
In the hallway for the Boots to clean.
I see it, in your version of this room,
Hanging on the wall, a byrnie of
Bright ring-a-lets, a trophy not of war,
But commerce, if in this mad world there is
A line between 'em!"
                                        wanting Christmas trees
And sleigh bells, wanting Father and his dollar
Bills, wanting Mother and her sip
Of champagne for him during dinner.

        "Satan shows the mean things,
            Denying him redemption
        As if it were his to offer.
        Offer! Offer me!
            The life of fun before the roast!"

No credit balance on the glass, no face
With knowing smirk, no glimpse of blood-dark seals
Upon a contract temptingly unrolled
As if it were a Persian rug – nothing,
Nothing broke the pallor of the glass.

"Offer me
The Future.
I will pay for *that*!"

It blazed, and only when he moved back far
Enough for focus could he see the passing
Chandeliers in endless hallways of
Kaleidoscopes whose snowflake shapes became
An ulcerated heart encased in scars
Like barnacles, and leaking blood with every
Beat, quivering on a field of scarlet
Mucus: Coat of Arms that sent him to
His knees, suppliant and terrified.
He clenched his fists and sought control. And when
He'd forced a note from shrill soprano down
To mellow bass, he rose, and made himself
A comforter at bedsides, friend to ragged
Indian children, deferential to
Old ladies, loader of collection-plates.

"Is it enough?
I *meant* benevolence.
Give me that, at least."

But the glass returned to silver, and
The room came up again, and he knew

How much he hated all these dusty relics
That his fathers had bequeathed him. Shouted,

"Ambiguity is the bottom rung of Courtesy!"

"The entrails of prophetic birds
Decay before your eyes. That
is their only message!"

"There are no crossroads. Only turnings!"

"We are weathercocks. Always facing upwind!"

The mirror brightened to a beach, on which
He saw a little girl whose hair blew glinting
In the sun as she walked away.

## THE POOL

Sindbad, always journeying,
Searching for his vanished mistress
Came one day upon a forest
Pool reflecting pines and silence.
"Here?" he asked in whispers, "Here?"
And a circle spread across
The surface of the vivid algae,
Something curious at his searching footfall.
He thought she'd touched her finger to
The surface from below and formed
A lens through which he might descry her
Smiling, silver-browed, the way she'd
Left him. But when he waded in
The circles from his ankles ran
Against her larger one as if
In combat; and the surface changed
To rippled glimmerings of trees,
Reflections of his folded chin
And dangling sausage fingers. This
Was what he'd done before: leaped
And landed all a-sprawl, erasing
In his awkwardness the careful
Truce-lines they had drawn between them.

## SEVEN COUPLETS WITH CROTCHETS
(or, *Why Models Grow Ugly*)

To begin with a face is a layer of skin
Covering nothing at all within.
 (Tongue and teeth don't count; they only kiss nourishment on its way through, and bones are just an ungraceful geometric diagram.)

Held out by cheekbones, stretched by nose,
Unstirred by action, limp in repose.
 (What can happen in a cradle? A splintery slat? A steaming drop of milk? What?)

Some faces are born with visual cues
That will a conditioned beholder bemuse.
 (Is the eye almond-shaped with pupil large and dark? Is the forehead round, the nose pugged? Will the mouth hold two spoons at once? Are the teeth Flat Omnivore, shiny to Love's taste as a Sweet? And the neck long-sloped beneath hair swaying in slow slow motion?)

That promise such languorous patrician delights
Life lived on elegant perfumed heights.
 (Breasts circles beneath a straight line, thighs that stretch longer than living limbs could; between neither will mortal ever lie, though he strive with the straining of an hundred laxatives, glisten with the gloss of a thousand hair oils, lave his armpits a millenium of mornings.)

But each day prods with molding thumb
Marking carefully what's to come.
    (Don't run. That thumb catches *everybody*!)

And if no resistance arises inside
Beauty sinks in to leathery hide.
    (Squeeze a rubber toy a million times: so, so. Now it
    snaps out more slowly, the paint comes off on fingers;
    cracks appear in creases that gape into leaks; and the
    demanding squeal of the valve fades into a despairing hiss.)

A proper filling trickles in
Of what you've seen and what you've been.
    (Grab 'em as they go by! bacon and Bacon and Bach; devour
    the books and smell the sunlight; treasure every touch of
    love, hoard each of hatred's hard agates; press it down
    'til you're as full as a Turkish-Napoleon-Armenian
    pastry, poly-delicious striated and smelling somewhat
    of lamb.)

## RAPTORES AND LOVECHICKS

You

            The Hawk

                                Plummeting
To clasp one tightly in the claws
Of contracts and agreements, leaving
But the head exposed from which
You'll pluck out every dangling curl
And disentangle every sweaty
                                        Love-bead;

You

            The Crow

                                All smiles across
The chess-board, planning moves, if not
For conquest, still to show that in
Societies of acquisition
Or defeat there may remain
A pleasing symmetry among
                                        The pieces;

You

            Wing-shot

                                By his indifference
To your trade or play, flutter
Down and join him. Pacifistics,
Patterns of a brocade jacket

In an acid-dream, mouths
Within marijuana tolling "Om,"
The wilting of a lotus in
Your navel's heat as high-tear-worthy
As the mortal sickness of
A child.

The air
A placid barn-yard
The ground
A sun-lit dust-hole
The sky
Paternal blue.
The Hen
Caught by the line drawn from her beak
The Goose
Half-foundered by its own pâté
The Turkey
Smug before Thanksgiving.

# DON JUAN SAYS FAREWELL

Oh my dear, they *all* are doomed, all the
Star-crossed, flag-decked, hen-tracked, gem-beblazoned,
Sweat-streaked Loves. All will wane and die
And fall in wrinkles, like a dry tea-bag.

Love begins to wilt beneath the blaze
Of streetlights, to shiver in chilly doorways,
To become bilious on buses and
Bloodshot at breakfast. Any heart
Must surely quail before voyeur desk-clerks
And prurient cab-drivers, and bare
Skin begins to prickle in the rhythms of
Strange beds. Hymeno Hymenea.

Each succeeding One has wrapped me in
A clinging silk cocoon, a chrysalis
Of muskèd scents, cleavages and clefts,
Binding blankets, button-bitten fingers,
Curling hair and hairs, freckle-finding,
Long and languid lunches, rumpled raiment,
Moist ear-filling sighs that thicken tongues,
Mammaries taut in elastic cups,
Scented shower-sweat beneath a robe,
Palpation of hard nipples and soft thighs,

The passages of a carnal maze,
A gummy trap, a fibrous gin that I
Must rend to pieces with a flaccid blade.

There is a waxing finality in
Each *post coitum triste*. (Do not blush,
My dear. Latin was once a tongue of Love
In spite of Ovid and Catullus), a
Wavering in the first-learned, favorite stance,
A febrile abhorrence of stainèd sheets
And the cold slide of contraceptives;
A shrinking from the stubble of her hot
Oppressive haunches as she shifts and snorts
In sated sleep, my substance caught between
The thighs that will, at last, conquer my loins.

No no, do not say that Love to me
Is only as the cagèd agile apes,
Careless of orifices, practise it.
If I were prone to images, cunning
Little *mots*, I could compare a Love
To a compost-heap that lies and ripens
'Neath the passing rain of years until
Amid its reeking mass, bright blooms appear.

But there have been no blooms for me.

Only the fondling of a thousand breasts
    That sagged into my hands as years drew on.
Only a morning tally of the liver-
    Spots that tattoo hands like a mocha scars;
Only careful work with brush and dye
    To cloak the head's emergence from its pelt.
Only an indifferent assurance
    That all our heady vows and protestations
Are no more than an insect's chittering
    As it goes about its raspy coupling;

That my tiny tumescence must retreat
Before the smallest whisper of the air
That lies in wait for me outside your bed;

That none of it can have the least import
Beside the lustral cycles of sun-spots,
The lunar debenture that holds the sea;

That we, poor quivering mites, are clustered on
A ball of warmth caught up in a galactic
Royal Progress; scrabbling on a gobbet

Of dung as we squeak and eat each other;
Poking here and there with eager paws,
All unmindful that we live in filth.

And so, indicative of where
I once began and soon must end, I wish
To lie alone in darkness, blank and warm.

## RECKLESS THROUGH THE ABZ'S

Reckless through the ABZ's, the child
Careens his toy fire-truck, and throws his ball,
Bespangled red-white-blue, against the wall
Until he misses; rummages the piled
Encrayoned picture-books to find the wild
Sore-wounded lion that befriends the tall
Explorer and his son. See, though small,
How sweet his playings are; for he, beguiled
In now, cannot conceive that pleasures end.
His father, then, the poorer? Knowing Death,
Despair, and sadness? Having more to spend
And less to buy? Hearing clocks portend
A final chiming? No. He knows that breath
Itself's an illness, which the dark will mend.

## THE ROCK-SKIPPER

In the morning
He threw the Perfect Rock, grained like tree-bark
And splashes high as fountains
Marched upon a distant island
Another
Perfect Opaline
And circles overlapped like drifting continents
Another
Ovoid and pudding-hued
Made its one great splash and then no more
Another
Thin and mica-specked
Curved up and vanished in the sun.
At last he threw the Perfect Nothing
And sat down upon the stones
Having learned that only children
        Throw such portents
        And read such auspices.

## THE PINK MONKEY

The Pink Monkey
    Swings in trees
Chanting in
    Strange litanies.

Singing from
    His own libretto
Wincing at
    His cracked falsetto.

Other monkeys
    Point and giggle
Inducing
    A shame-faced wriggle.

Other monkeys
    Point and snicker
Saying they'll
    Get richer quicker.

Other monkeys
    Fondling bricks
Summon him
    For "Pick-Up-Sticks."

Poor Pink Monkey!
    How he's tried
To find some way
    To tan his hide.

STATIONS OF THE ZOO

*THE ELEPHANT*

Passing: A rolling ship in an ocean swell.
Approaching: Earth-skin rolled back underfoot.
Facing: A jet refueling on peanuts.

*THE PENGUIN*

What formal banquet goes he to
Reeking so of fish?

*THE LION: NOIL EHT*

Peanut-vendors.
Pink balloons, Children
Stinks (Popcorn Cherry-
Urine-pop) Hummock
Buildings. Dung-strewn floor.
Chilly meat. Attendants squirting hoses

Tail-eluding flies.
Sleep. Dry savannah.
Heat-shimmer. Torn hid
Marrow-bones. Waddling
Vultures. Long-beak birds.
High-back hyenas. Giant sun

We see a Library Lion Couchant.

*HUMMING-BIRDS, TOUCANS, COCKS-OF-THE-ROCK, ROLLOVER*

Frenetic Gems
Fled from a living necklace.

*MACAW TO ANSWER OR IMITATE*

The Man nods his head. So (Blue) does the Macaw.
The Man gives three caracoles. So (Red) does the Macaw.
The Man laughs and laughs. So (Green) does the Macaw.

## *THE GORILLA*

His belly lolling on cement
He sits and ponders what he meant,
This fellow Darwin.

Their talk is scanty evidence
To prove the ones outside the fence
Truly *are* Men.

## *"MOST BEAUTIFUL AND EXCESSIVELY KIND"*

(–from "*The Bestiary*")

The Panther, whom I saw in sleep,
Latterly raised his head
And belched a cloud of sweet Allspice
To strike a Dragon dead.

Claws of silver, eyes of gold
Ebon-black of coat
No feral rumble came from him
But a sweeter note

As he told of things that Panthers know
In a voice of singing bells
May I sometime find again
The dream where that Creature dwells.

## TEN THINGS I WILL NOT DO

I
Interrupt my daughter's teacher

II
Wish brown grass green

III
Collect!
Sand-grains in a snuffbox
Beans in a jar
Money

IV
Leave a footprint in
Asphalt
Peat
Piecrust
Water

V
Count the stars in an interstice of leaves

VI
Think about John Keats

VII
Decide which is "Will not"
And what is "Must not"

VIII
Erase my signature

IX
Wave (back) at a meteor-flare

X
Answer your question

## THE TOY MONKEY

Someone's gift, the box was gaily wrapped
In Oriental paper. The directions
Ended with three glyphs I took to be
Japanese. The fur was false, soft,
And brown; the eyes brown with startling yellow
Irises. A place to press brought it
Alive. It knuckled to a chair and up.
Its head turned left right left right.
Its orange muzzle opened as to speak.
'A Talking Toy' so I said "Hello!"
Close to the head. "Hello!" it answered back.
I laughed and tickled his stomach-fur with
A finger, and he wiggled and said "Hello!"
Curious, I removed the head
And looked:  springs and lever, spool of tape,
And a set of batteries.
                                        What sort
Of pet would a real monkey have been? Why,
Perhaps to eat and bleed and snap at guests.
But this was more a small slow child that held
My finger when we walked about the room,
Or, on my shoulder, clutched my head with dry-furred
Arms. I taught his tape to say "Idiot!"
And "Crimentilees!" and "Thus I refute

Berkeley," and he would play in his stiff way,
Shambling through the rooms a-chittering,
Making queer designs with shredded paper,
Staring through the windows at the children.
Then, as if he needed warmth, he'd clamber
In my lap and seem to go to sleep,
Although the yellow eyes could never close.
How long his life? How long those batteries?
At night I turned him off, and put him in
A little bed I'd bought. But every day
The time required to wake became a little
Longer. Once I went away a week,
And, turned on again on my return,
Four hours passed before he recognized me,
As if the exile from his power source
(whatever it may have been) left him lifeless.
I could have changed his batteries, I suppose,
But what he was was what I loved, waning
Though it was. One night he played no more:
Sat waiting on the couch for me to sit,
Climbed into my lap and curling up
Said, "Tired" (a word I'd never taught him), stopped,
Slept. The pressing-place elicited
A hum, a twitch. I put him gently in
A closet out of sight, and threw out the bed.
                                        Does he dream? Do I?

## THREE SILHOUETTES

### I

### *GREAT-GRANDFATHER MATT*

He wore tall hats
With symmetrical dents and the brim
turned down all 'round

Traded cattle in Missouri
'til his horse ran off
and threw him from his buggy

Never woke before they put the stone
above his head to keep him down

A gray stone, arched like a church-window
which his wife
Still could find with flowers
when her eyes had failed.

I think of him in his muttonchop whiskers
like runaway earmuffs
And wonder what he would have made
of nails of stainless steel
And marbly beef in plastic wrap
Or Daddy's Model-A, which
he couldn't urge on with
the lightest of loving whip-flicks.

II

*GREAT-UNCLE MATT*
AND

Grandaddy ran the farm
Buried dirty dishes in the backyard
Played Euchre on the porch 'til after dark
Trained a turkey-gobbler as a watchdog

WHEN

Grandaddy got married
Matt said " 'Bye!"
Moved to Atlanta and went into insurance

MARRIED ONCE
at forty-four

When his twenty-year-old wife died
Came home to live in a vacant tenant-house
Sat evenings with a horse-pistol
Firing through the ceiling
at squirrels in the attic
If the squirrels were absent
Spiders would do

## III

### *UNCLE JOE, HIS ARM ACROSS A HORSE'S NECK*

When I knew him, Uncle Joe
Parted his hair straight down the middle
Wore overalls and rubber boots
And kept a bottle in the barn
        To get through milking in the morning

His stepson mocked him constantly
Called him "Rummy" and hid his shoes
Washed and waxed his car, and cried
When Uncle Joe said, "Thanks a lot.
Thanks a lot. Thanks a lot.
        Thanks a lot. Thanks a lot."

## AUTUMN

Now, beneath that same bright sky that snarled
With sullen heat before, a frigid whistling
Wind races the clouds (fleeing bands of white)
Across the watering eye. On the beach
The cold-numbed nose strains for scent of sea,
And the waves glint as icy blue as crumpled
Christmas foil. On the street the walker wears
A sweater with his short-sleeved shirt. The dog
Sleeps sunward, wind-spots stirring in his fur.
Summer, still drowsy at her dismissal,
Drops her brush, and leaves the hills half-green.

## 25 BLACKOUTS 25

Six cats doing their nails with orange-sticks.
Face relected hind-part-to and upside down in the bathwater.
A raincloud weeping urine.
Two swizzle-sticks tied in a love-knot
    Dancing widdershins around an eggplant.
Seven dogs playing violins with dental floss.
Walling up a cask of Amontillado.
Eight-legged words without mouths.
A world-globe inside out.
Patulous and pendulous, elephants.
Eight iguanas plaited in a hangman's noose.
Taking a foul-shot with the planet Mars.
Wearing a marble head with argent eyes.
All the streets together spelling "Love."
Through your ribs, the Sun.
Treading a waterwheel upstream.

A mantis polishing its glasses.
Two breasts with nipples kissing smack smack.
Using a broadsword for a baton.
Raining upward, rinsing roots.
Quartet of mustachioed geologists singing "This Flatulent Earth"
A traffic-cop directing hummingbirds.
Hippopotamus hiccoughing without apology.
Up the street comes a little pink man
    Picking his nose and peeing in a can
    Long his ears and short his legs
Pirouetting on squeaking eggs.
Toy airplane smoke-writing THE END.

## ABOUT THE AUTHOR . . .

ROBERT L. SMITH has published poetry in some thirty-five magazines, including *Shenandoah*, *The Beloit Poetry Journal*, *Discourse*, *The Western Humanities Review*, *The Georgia Review*, and the *Wisconsin Review*. "Journeys and Changes," which first appeared in *The Little Magazine*, was selected for the 1974 Borestone Mountain Poetry Awards volume, *Best Poems of 1973*. He has been twice a guest at Yaddo. He is a member of the Poetry Society of America. Currently he is teaching English at the Bronx High School of Science in New York City.

*(Photo by Steve See)*